How to Tell If Your House Is Haunted

And what to do if it is

Lee Allen Howard

THREE FIRST NAMES

Jamestown, NY

HOW TO TELL IF YOUR HOUSE IS HAUNTED:
AND WHAT TO DO IF IT IS

Published by *Three First Names. Cover design by Three First Names.*

ISBN: 0692595473   ISBN-13: 978-0692595473

Contact the author at: https://leeallenhoward.com

Also by Lee Allen Howard

- *Can You Be a Christian Medium?*
- *Mediumship and Its Laws* by Hudson Tuttle
- *God's World: A Treatise on Spiritualism* by the William T. Stead Memorial Center
- *The Next Room* by Doris and Hilary Severn
- *Letters from Heaven* by Clarissa A. Sprague
- *Death Perception*
- *Desperate Spirits*
- *The Adamson Family*
- *Speaking in Tongues*
- *Tongues Are for You! How to Release Your Prayer Language*
- *The Conception of Jesus*
- *Manifestations Throughout Church History*
- *Called and Commissioned: 14 Principles for Budding Prophets*
- *Prosper the Bible Way*
- *Get Outta Debt!*
- *How to Be Carefree*
- *The Dream of the Institutional Church*

https://leeallenhoward.com

Praise for Lee Allen Howard

"Dastardly devious, cleverly conceived, and just a whole lot of fun to read, *Death Perception* is Lee Allen Howard on fire and at his finest. Rife with winsome weirdness, it's like the mutant stepchild of Carl Hiaasen and Stephen King, mixing a truly unique paranormal coming-of-age story with a quirky cast of offbeat noir characters into a novel that's simply unforgettable... and hilariously original. A supernatural crime story, blazing with creative intrigue... don't miss it."
　　　　　　　　　—Michael Arnzen, author of *Play Dead*

"Lee Allen Howard's *Death Perception* is a red hot union of Gothic crime thriller and grim humor that burns with supernatural tension. Beneath the sickly sweet scent of caramelized sugar lies the wildly entertaining tale of a man who delivers justice to the dead while fanning the fires of the living. Ever hear the expression, 'laughing in a morgue'? Death Perception feels just like that. Howard has a gift for crafting eccentric characters and clever plots. This is dark fun at its best."
　　　　　—Jason Jack Miller, author of *The Devil and Preston Black*
　　　　　　　　　　　　　　　　　　　and *Hellbender*

"*Death Perception* has officially made me envious of Lee Allen Howard. It sings like a choir of angels, while weeping like a ghost in winter. Everyone should have this in their collection."
　　　　　　　　—Trent Zelazny, author of *To Sleep Gently*
　　　　　　　　　　　　　　　　　　　and *Butterfly Potion*

How to Tell If Your House Is Haunted

And what to do if it is

Contents

"Beloved, do not believe every spirit,
but test the spirits to see whether they
are from God..."
—*1 JOHN 4:1 NRSV*

Sympathy for the dead

You're dead and you don't know it. Or, for whatever reason, you can't move on toward the light. Maybe you had a hard life followed by an untimely or wrongful death. Perhaps a violent death. Your body is gone—buried or lost—and long since decayed. Even your etheric body has dissolved, finally freeing what's left: your astral body, your soul.

Free to roam about the astral plane, a realm that pervades the physical, you continue to experience the thoughts and feelings you did while you were still physically incarnated.

After a distressing life that ended in perhaps a less-than-peaceful death, these emotions draw you to return to the locations where you formed these memories: the place of your death... your home... some favorite haunt.

Years pass.

Your family and friends die. New owners claim the prop-erty you used to live on, the house you once inhabited. Strangers invade your home. They change things. And ignore you.

Sometimes it's hard to see the living through the mist.

Yet when you do, you try to get their attention. You speak to them, touch them. But other than a brief puzzled look, they fail to acknowledge you.

You try, and try again. You succeed in finally gaining their notice. *But they're frightened... horrified.* They talk about you in the worst way, as if you're not even there.

This certainly isn't what you wanted or expected.

This may go on for decades, and the players may change. But you remain, repeating the same interactions.

Until someone seeks to contact you.

Sadly, they treat it like a game. Or because they've become so frightened—you can't understand why trying to get their attention is so harrowing—they invite a priest to cast you out like some unclean demon. Or worse, they call in a team of paranormal investigators to root you out and evict you.

This, perhaps, is what it's like for a departed spirit still lingering on the earth plane.

I watched over fifty episodes of a cable TV channel's popular psychic investigation show in the span of a week. I was struck with the investigators' disrespect for those who have passed yet remain ensnared in the lower astral realms.

It's nice to tell these souls to move on or to hold an impromptu memorial service in the final two minutes of the show, but what's with all the challenges to "show yourself," along with name calling? I understand ghost hunters want to provoke spirits to manifest themselves. If they do, it proves their presence so that investigators can establish evidence of genuine paranormal activity.

But what if you were on the other side of that kind of treatment? How would it make you feel?

On this side of death or the other, spirits are still *people.* A lingering spirit is a fellow human who died but simply failed to advance from the lower realms, for whatever reason. Such beings don't usually remain here because they were happy, blessed, and well-adjusted in their physical life. They may have suffered a troubling transition.

To be bullied by ghost-hunters adds insult to injury. Granted, some departed individuals are bullies too. But not all of them.

Whether lingering spirits are sweet or bitter, do we have the right to be rude? We may be frightened at their presence and misunderstand the signs they offer, but it doesn't mean they seek to harm or scare.

As I continued to view episodes of the television program, this message about the departed became clear. I wanted to communicate their plight. It's as if a whole roomful of departed spirits were watching with me and urging me to write something in their defense.

More than anything, departed souls want to be *understood.* I hope this little book helps.

In the next chapter, I'll share some alternative ways to handle paranormal activity.

Test the spirits

Experiencing paranormal activity is naturally startling—sometimes frightening. The unknown and unexpected can evoke fear.

However, simply because you're alarmed doesn't mean the activity is malicious.

Unless ongoing paranormal activity causes actual harm, you would do well to analyze the events.

Here are four suggestions about how to evaluate unexplained phenomena.

1. Is the activity truly paranormal?

There are many explanations for strange portents.

Thirty years ago, I suffered disturbed sleep, sitting bolt upright every night at 3:00 a.m., the hour known as "dead time" among some paranormal researchers. I wondered if I was being awakened by a spirit because it was so remarkably regular.

Turns out that right before I went to bed at 11:00 p.m., I was in the habit of taking a Sudafed—the little red four-hour pill—which, when it wore off (at 3:00 a.m.), woke me like an alarm clock. This is a common reaction to the medication. Certainly not paranormal.

Ensure what you're experiencing has no natural explanation.

If you feel sick at home or in certain rooms, check the carbon monoxide level there. If you're anxious, feel like you're being watched, or get "creeped out" in particular spots, check for a source of high EMF (electromagnetic field) from any appliances, electrical devices, or wiring in that area. You can purchase an EMF tester from an electronics store or online retailer.

Rule out natural sources before you go hunting for a ghost.

2. Is the activity interactive?

Like the community fire department testing their fire whistle every Wednesday at noon, some paranormal events are merely repetitive energy signals that follow a cycle. If you're not present to experience them every time, it's hard to determine if a pattern exists.

Although such psychic imprints are considered paranormal, they are not necessarily produced by departed spirits. They are remnants of psychic or astral energy that are tied to places and repeat regularly or when they are triggered, like a motion-activated outdoor light. This kind of phenomena is not truly interactive.

However, if you ask specific questions and get answers in the form of whispers, tapping, knocking, moving objects, you may be experiencing interaction with some kind of spirit or energy being.

3. Is the activity increasing?

Whenever I become aware of some new phenomenon occurring, I seek to determine the source. I admit that once a certain reason suggests itself to me, it's harder to entertain alternative explanations. So make sure you seek answers to the previous two questions.

If you believe the activity is paranormal *and* interactive, **consider whether it's increasing in frequency.**

Early after I've first noticed a phenomenon, I may believe it's escalating when what's actually increasing is my *sensitivity and attentiveness* to occurrences that are happening at their typical rate.

A good way to determine whether activity is mounting is to journal or chart the experiences: note the date, time, circumstances, and a description of each event. Over the course of a few weeks or months, analyze your data for trends and then make a decision.

If activity actually is increasing, it could be that something is trying to get your attention and is doubling its efforts because you've responded. Just as likely, there could be some reason for the increase that you don't yet understand.

Part of keeping an open mind is not jumping to conclusions.

4. Is the activity malicious?

After you've ruled out natural causes for the phenomenon and determined that it *is* interactive, it's time to ask if the activity is malicious, meant to harm.

If you've been threatened audibly (*"Get out… GET OUT!"*) or physically hurt (hit, pushed), it's easy to determine that the activity is harmful.

But, as stated previously, **simply because an occurrence is startling or frightening doesn't make it malicious.**

Sure, no one likes being awakened at 3:00 a.m. or touched on the shoulder when alone in a dark room, or continually picking up knick-knacks that won't stay on the mantel.

Yet, if you were a spirit in a home you once owned and wanted to interact with the current inhabitants, what might you do to get their attention? If you were a departed child and you were bored and merely wanted to play, what would you do to interest a playmate?

Because the living typically cannot see or hear departed spirits, reaction to breakthrough contact could be less than pleasant—for either party. If you tried to get someone's attention to talk to them because you were lonely and they reacted by screaming, how would you feel?

If you think it's a spirit…

Just like responding to physically living individuals, **how you react to spirit contact is up to you.** If you see it as something fearful and negative, it will be.

We are conditioned to believe that ghosts are spooky, that the paranormal is undesirable. Sometimes it is. But usually, it's simply different from what we're used to in our physical, day-to-day existence.

Although experiencing paranormal phenomena may be discomforting, can you withhold judgment about it until you've tested it? Without impulsively pigeon-holing it as good/bad, holy/evil?

In the next chapter, we'll discuss whether you should make contact and how to do it.

Contacting spirits

Once you've determined that the activity you're experiencing is paranormal as well as interactive, based on your objectives, you may want to communicate with the entity.

Should you make contact with a spirit?

I must stress here that **I do *not* recommend using spirit boards (Ouija or others) to contact spirit entities.** I've heard little good coming from such contact, which can open the door for more serious harassment or oppression.

Those departed souls still lingering on the border of the physical world are in the lowest astral realm (see "The lower astral levels" on page 22). Just as you would not make friends on the worst street corners of the city, it's unwise to seek relationship with lingering spirits. Many are benign—but not all.

What to do if the activity is malicious

If you've determined that the activity is interactive and malicious, reasoning with such entities—human or otherwise—may prove ineffective. If you think the malevolent activity is non-human in origin, consider enlisting professional help from a qualified paranormal investigator or clergy member.

Ridding your home of spirit boards and questionable fetish objects (such as voodoo dolls) is also a good start.

In the meantime, you may want to burn sage leaves, which is a cleansing incense (do so carefully). If you're so inclined, the "Daily prayer and mediation" on page 53 and the "Daily prayer and mediation" on page 53. Keep reading for more tips.

What to do if the entity is benign

If you believe the activity is from a departed human spirit, you may want to contact the entity to set some boundaries or encourage them to leave.

Departed spirits are still the same people they were in their previous incarnation. They don't automatically become all-wise and saintly just because they've entered the afterworld. Neither do they become malicious devils.

Christopher Penczak states in his book *Spirit Allies*:

> Ghosts and apparitions do not seem to know any more of the secrets of life than the living. Their perspective has not changed, only their body has ceased. They are still in the physical realm.

Granted, if they're stuck in the lower astral realms from which they occasionally appear in the physical, they're possibly dealing with some kind of trauma that has kept them from advancing into the higher realms: wrongful or violent death, concern for those they've left behind, or some unfinished business.

So, in some sense, many such lingering spirits are dys-functional entities. (This is no different from the living we encounter—even members of our own families.) Treat them accordingly.

Making contact with spirits

If you've done your due diligence to determine the nature of the paranormal activity and decided that the contact is inter-active and human, it's time to address the issue.

After you've done any spiritual housecleaning and entreated the help of spiritual allies, you may simply speak out loud to the spirits. A good time is when you encounter activ-ity; you know they're near.

Your key stance: **Don't be afraid.**

1. Stand up to malicious spirits

If it seems to be a bullying entity, stand up to it and tell it you won't accept that kind of treatment any longer. But do it in such a way that doesn't provoke unnecessary harassment.

Don't be flip. As you would deal with the living, **be respectful yet firm**.

2. Acknowledge benign spirits

Spirits are still people, and they want to be recognized, remembered, understood, and respected.

First of all, acknowledge their presence. *"I know you're here. Do you want to communicate with me?"*

Realize they can probably hear you, although you may be unable to hear them. Pay attention, though, to the thoughts you receive, the impressions and feelings you experience.

3. Lay the ground rules

Communicate your desires, whatever they may be.

If you think you can peacefully cohabit with the entities, tell them so, but explain what they may and may not do in your presence: *"You are not allowed to wake me up in the middle of the night anymore. No more scaring the kids."* Set the parameters for whatever applies to your situation.

You may want to inform them there's something bet-ter waiting for them—that it's time to move on. Tell them to go toward the light, to accept the help of those who would escort them higher. Here's what psychic Marisa Anderson said to "clean" a house:

> "You need to know that you are dead. You've been dead for a very long time and we are here to help you now. Just understand that you are dead. ... Can you see the light? [Go to the light.]"

—Elaine Mercado, *Grave's End* (2001)

4. Tell them to leave

If you want to give the spirits a trial period to test their coop-eration, you can. However, if their activity is disturbing now or later, simply tell them to leave. *"I acknowledge your interest in me/us, but it's unwelcome. You need to move on. You must leave this place now."*

Again, **be firm yet courteous**. Penczak advises,

> If beings do not come in love, ask them to leave by the [power of your deity] three times. Send them unconditional love and light. Visualize white light in your home space. One who is not in the light will

either go toward it or shun it and leave. You cannot force harmful spirits into the light, but there is no need to put up with them. You can only request they go and show them the way.

—*Spirit Allies*

5. Be persistent

It may take more than once for departed spirits to get the message. Stand your ground and insist that they leave. You have the authority to do so; believe it!

I would love to know how this works for you. Please reach out to me (see "About the author" on page 55).

May God bless you and bring peace, love, and light to you and your home.

Keep reading for bonus material…

Bonus Material

What happens when you die

Death is the one experience we'll all one day face, whether we're ready or not. But the final transition need not be the "great mystery" it's often made out to be. Toward a practical understanding, this chapter explains what happens when we die.

People end physical life in a variety of ways: naturally, accidentally, expectedly, unexpectedly. At the end of a full term or, in the opinion of some, much too soon.

Yet no matter how the end is reached, most transition experiences share ten elements, identified by Dr. Raymond Moody in *Life After Life* (1975).

Your possible transition

The following is a composite experience that contains all the elements, which I will list afterward.

Whether from an extended illness or a sudden trauma, you are dying.

As you reach the turning point where your physical body can no longer sustain life, you hear someone—a doctor, a loved one—pronounce that you are dead. A ringing or buzz-

17

ing sound follows. You feel yourself speeding through a long, dark tunnel.

Then you find yourself outside of your physical body in the place where you've died. A silver cord connecting the back of your head to your physical body snaps and retracts. **You are surprised to see your own body lying there, feel strange to be a spectator from a vantage point you've never before experienced.** Perhaps you observe others exerting themselves to resuscitate you. Or maybe a loved one is there, mourning your passing, and this may trouble you emotionally. But after some time, you adjust to the situation and accept this different experience.

You discover that you still have a body but notice it's different from the one you've vacated. You find you have new abilities. You can move at the impulse of desire.

Wondering whether you're alone in your newfound state, others suddenly appear, and you somehow know they've come to help you. You're pleased to realize they're the spirits of relatives and friends who have passed on before you—sometimes many years ago: your parents or grandparents, a lifelong friend or other supporter.

With them is a being you don't recognize, and whose kind you've never met on the earthly plane. But this soul of light is incredibly kind and loving, and you are extremely comforted by its presence.

No one speaks—at least not with their mouths. Communication happens by transfer of thought, and you find this fascinating.

The being of light engages you in a dialogue, and together you begin to review your life. This thought-conversation is accompanied by a panoramic playback of the primary events of your life. But it's an objective review, without distress or judgment concerning the presentation. From it, you gain a new perspective on the meaning of your physical existence and the lessons you learned.

While you've been engaged in the cinematic review of your incarnation, you find that you've moved with your companion to a new setting, what you sense is the borderline that separates the natural world from the next realm. You are overcome with intense feelings of love, joy, and peace.

With your spirit guide, you cross over into a countryside whose beauty you've only imagined in your sweetest dreams. And more loved ones are there to greet you. As you move through the gate of light, you understand that this is now your home.

Ten elements of transition

This composite scenario includes the following elements, events that most transitional experiences share:

1. Hearing the pronouncement of death or realizing that you have died.
2. Feeling a newfound peace and quiet.
3. Hearing the roaring noise that accompanies the spirit vacating the body.
4. Seeing the dark tunnel, which is the visual counterpart of the roaring noise as the spirit leaves the body through the crown of the head. The "silver cord" is severed.
5. Being out of the body and discovering new super-physical abilities.
6. Meeting other spirit beings known (or known of) during earthly life.

7. Engaging with the being of light.

8. Experiencing your life review.

9. Reaching the border between the physical and spiritual worlds.

10. Crossing over into the Summerland, the land of love and light.

Now you know what to expect when you inevitably reach the end of physical life. You will shed your body, be greeted by loved ones, and transition into the world of Spirit with the help of a being of light.

Although it will be a new experience, it needn't be feared. Compared to a brief sojourn on the earthly plane, Spirit is our true home, one whose beauty is to be enjoyed for eternity.

Where do we go when we die?

A brief overview of the astral realms and above

As spiritual beings, our presence in the physical, earthly world is only a temporary sojourn. We existed before we incarnated in this lifetime, and we will continue to exist after our mortal bodies die and return to dust.

But *where* will we exist?

Christian-based and other religions claim that those who have lived righteous lives "go to heaven." Yet, what *is* heaven?

Spiritualist, Theosophical, and New Age sources teach that when we die, our souls (our surviving energy bodies with our consciousness and personal identity) enter what is called the *astral realm*.

What is the astral realm?

In *Handbook to the Afterlife*, Pamela Rae Heath and Jon Klimo define the astral realm:

> **Astral:** A multilevel nonphysical reality that is said to exist beyond the physical realm, where human beings are said to go following the death of their

physical body. Sometimes called the *bardo*, this is where spirits dwell between their incarnations or after they have finished incarnating.

As there are many social strata in mortal earth life, a number of levels exist in the astral realm. I've depicted these planes in the following diagram.

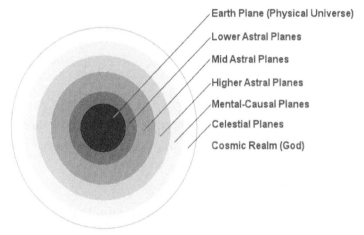

Earth Plane (Physical Universe)
Lower Astral Planes
Mid Astral Planes
Higher Astral Planes
Mental-Causal Planes
Celestial Planes
Cosmic Realm (God)

The Planes of Existence

Let's look briefly at each of these planes.

The lower astral levels

Heath and Klimo explain that, "Lower levels of the astral, close to the earth plane, are said to be dark and unpleasant locations with a 'heavy' or 'dense' level of vibration." Those who have consistently lived wicked lives, maliciously harming themselves and others, rejecting any spark of light or higher values may find themselves here.

The **lowest level** is dark and gloomy. It is a realm of negative emotions and dark vices that cannot be satisfied because the inhabitants no longer have physical bodies. It's like purgatory. *But it is not eternal*; those who work through their issues and learn to forsake their negative thoughts and evil desires are able to move upward with the aid of those who come to instruct and help them.

In the afterlife, you gravitate toward the level your thoughts and actions in earth life have warranted.

The level above the lowest is much like earth in its scenery, but its inhabitants may not realize they're dead. Or they may hold some fear or belief about the afterlife that prevents them from rising into the higher realms.

Again, existence in this realm is not permanent. **All souls can go higher if they desire to grow and advance.**

The middle astral levels

Populating the **middle levels** are those who are busy fulfilling the intellectual desires and aspirations they were unable to manifest fully in earth life. If you never got an opportunity to master your favorite subject on earth, you'll have another chance here.

Moving upward, there's a level where the inhabitants are reliving scenes of ancient peoples, reenacting and experiencing the lives that they once enjoyed—or were fascinated with—on the earth plane. The scenery here is created by the imagination of the participants.

The dwellers in the **upper mid astral realm** are engaged in useful, inventive, and constructive work. Here they perfect what their professional or occupational interests were when they lived on earth. Artist, musicians, architects, scientists, doctors, craftspeople are busy creating their masterpieces here.

The mid astral realm is what Spiritualists refer to as "the Summerland."

The upper astral levels

The higher astral realms are those of ideology, philosophy, and religion. The **penultimate plane** is where "religious aspirations and emotions find their full power of expression" (Rick Richards).

The **highest astral plane** is inhabited by the great scientists, philosophers, and metaphysicians of all time. Highly evolved beings descend from higher realms to teach those who have attained this highest astral plane.

What lies beyond the astral planes?

The highest realms of existence

Beyond the astral realm is the **mental-causal plane**, where selfless individuals of advanced evolution cooperate to bring spiritual enlightenment to the lower realms as well as earth.

> Supposedly all great inventions, religious and moral progressions, spiritual leadership and so on, come from here, inspired by beings who were once on Earth but have had the opportunity to increase their talents in the afterlife.
>
> —Near-Death Experiences & the Afterlife

The **celestial realm**, according to psychic researcher Frederic W. H. Myers, is a realm of light. Beings on this level have evolved through all aspects of the created universe. They have fulfilled their unique purpose in the evolution of consciousness and now exist as beings of light without form. Ascended figures such as Jesus and Buddha are said to dwell here.

The highest realm, the cosmic, is the abode of what we call God, the Source, or Infinite Intelligence. Little can be said about this realm because it simply cannot be communicated. But it is the point from which creation originated, and to which all things will eventually return.

These are the realms that will one day be our home. Let us aspire to attain the best in this life that we may reach the highest in the next.

Will you know it when you die?

It's important to cultivate a faith in the afterlife, an assurance that consciousness and identity continue after the change called physical death. For, no matter what your belief is, the eternality of the soul is a reality.

Those who are unacquainted with what happens after the soul leaves behind the body at physical death—and especially those who disbelieve in an afterlife—sometimes find themselves in perplexing circumstances.

To disembodied souls, the "soul body" is **just as physical and solid to them as their physical bodies were**, and instead of moving on (because they don't know they're supposed to), they remain on the earth plane among people who are still physically embodied.

The only problem is that disembodied souls usually cannot make themselves seen or heard by those still living. When loved ones and helpers in the spirit world come to escort them away from the physical realm, they refuse to go because they don't believe they are "dead" (physically) and have no concept or belief in an afterlife.

The danger for these souls is becoming stuck on the earth

plane instead of progressing to the joys of life in the higher astral realms.

The plight of Geoffrey

Gladys Osborne Leonard

The following is an account told by British trance medium **Gladys Osborne Leonard** (1882–1968) in Susy Smith's *She Speaks to the Dead: The Life of Gladys Osborne Leonard* (New York: Award Books, 1972). It's about a civilian named Geoffrey, who died in a bombing in World War II.

> Geoffrey was killed during an air raid. His mother came to Gladys soon afterward in an effort to get in touch with him, and it wasn't long before communication was well established. He told his

mother what had happened just after the bomb fell
on the building in which he lived.

He seemed to have been unconscious for a time,
then he became aware of a pleasant lightness of body
and cheerfulness of mind—a feeling that all was well
with him such as he had never experienced before.
For a little while he basked in this happy state of
well-being. Then he realized that he was lying on the
ground, amid a scene of desolation and destruction.
An unknown voice whispered to him, "Don't be
disturbed or distressed at what you see around you.
Detach yourself from it, then you can free yourself
and come away with us to where you belong. You
have no connection now with these conditions."

"Yes, I *am* connected with them," he answered.
"I can't leave them. There's something I must do
here. I must pull myself together and find out what's
happened."

And he turned away from the unseen helper and
tried to think what he must do. As he looked at
the debris around him he began to recall hearing
a tremendous noise. Then the full memory of the
air raid came back to him. It seemed extraordinary
to him that he felt no pain. Surely he must have
been injured, but he obviously wasn't. As he had
often watched the wounded being carried away on
stretchers after an air raid, feeling sorry for their sad
plight, he now had an intense sense of relief at his
own escape.

He thought of his mother and wished to see her
as quickly as possible in order to let her know that
he was not only alive but uninjured; he got up and
walked to the corner of the next street, where he
usually met her. When she wasn't there, he waited

some time. Then, although he found it difficult to
fit the most natural and simple ideas together in
his mind, he finally recalled that she'd gone to the
country for a few days. There was nothing to do
but wait for her return, but he wondered where he
should go to spend the night, since his building
was demolished. Seeing two people he knew, he
approached them.

Geoffrey had always been somewhat reserved—
liked and respected, but not in the habit of forming
close friendships easily. The few people who knew
him well valued his friendship and responded
warmly to it, so **he was quite perplexed when he got
no response from these friends to his greetings**. He
repeated them several times over, still with no effect.
Beginning to feel worried, he stood squarely in front
of the person he addressed, but he apparently was
not seen. His friends seemed to look through him,
not at him. As he walked away sadly, he watched
others moving with difficulty through the rubble
on the street, feeling their way carefully; he realized
with considerable shock that the blackout hour
had arrived and, while it was evidently quite dark
for them, to him it was light enough to distinguish
objects and persons clearly.

Geoffrey began to wonder whether he was really
as uninjured as he had thought. Perhaps he had
sustained a concussion. He felt very lonely and
rather frightened; he decided to do the sensible
thing and go straight to a hospital. There he went
up to a man on duty at the entrance desk and
immediately began in a concise way to explain his
condition. **The man took absolutely no notice of
him.** He didn't even look up from his work, although

Geoffrey began shouting at him to get his attention. Then the man got up and walked out through a doorway at the back of the room, leaving him alone and unnoticed and almost in a state of panic. In his extremity he closed his eyes and sent out a fervent prayer, an entreaty wrung from the very depths of his soul.

Almost immediately he became aware that healing hands touched him, took hold of him in a reassuring way. He felt content to surrender himself to the ministrations of these unseen friends and had no wish to open his eyes again, nor had he any curiosity regarding his helpers' identity. He drifted into a deep sleep, giving himself up to the feeling of peace and safety that now filled him.

After a time Geoffrey awoke. He wanted to move about, to know where he was, and who the people were who surrounded him. He began to realize that many of those with him were his relatives and friends… but they were all people who had died! He thought of course that he was dreaming. **Many have this reaction at first, when they are unprepared for the conditions they will find after death.** In time, however, he began to wonder why his dream was lasting so long. Thinking about his mother, he stirred in an effort to move and get things done.

His anxiety was sensed by those around him, and a restraining hand was placed on his shoulder. He found himself looking into the face of a man whose expression was full of understanding and kindness, combined with a dignity of bearing that was most impressive. As Geoffrey gazed inquiringly into his face, he realized that the features were like those in an old photograph his mother had. Even before the stranger spoke and identified himself, Geoffrey was aware that this must be his father, who had died when he was an infant.

It was his father who told him that he had left his physical body forever. He would not return to it because it had been rendered useless and beyond repair, through the injuries he had received in the recent air raid.

A terrible longing for his mother seized Geoffrey when he began to consider how she would mourn for him. He yearned to tell her that he wasn't really dead after all. At the same time, he eagerly set about getting to know his father and adjusting himself to his new environment. Almost the first thing he asked, however, was if it would be possible for him to get in touch with his mother to let her know he was still alive and well.

He was told that unless he was able to get through to her directly—and that would depend on her receptivity to him—the only means of communication was through a medium. He drew back somewhat at that. He had always been so reserved that it would be difficult for him to tell a stranger of his intimate love for his mother so that his concern could be transmitted to her. Yet even though his mother undoubtedly possessed natural psychic gifts because of her artistic and sensitive nature and would probably be more responsive to spirit influence than most people, it still might be hard for him to impress her at just the right moment, when she herself was in the proper mood. Her natural grief would cause her such distress that it was doubtful whether she could provide the necessary relaxed condition for psychic receptivity.

Geoffrey found this to be only too true when, later, he made his first attempt to speak to her. By then he'd had so many wonderful experiences in his new life that he longed to tell her about them. As he concentrated his thought on her and found himself beside her, he realized that his fears about her reaction to the news of his death were quite correct.

She lay on her bed crying. He knelt beside her, putting his arms around her and holding her to him, but there was no response. Her frail body shook with the violence of her grief; he could not get through to her in any way. It was difficult for him not to react to her emotion but he sternly forced himself into a calm frame of mind, which his father had explained to him he must do if he was to impress her with his presence. He prayed quietly yet fervently that the power would be given him to penetrate her anguish and afford her some measure of consolation. Gradually she ceased her sobbing, then raised herself on her elbows and looked around inquiringly. A dawning look of surprise, lit by the faintest ray of hope, came over her features, and she whispered inquiringly, wonderingly, beseechingly, "Geoff?"

He continued trying to impress her with a feeling of assurance as to the reality of his presence and his love for her. She seemed to receive something of this and said again, "Geoff?" Then she added, "Geoff, are you here? Is it really you? Speak to me if it's you."

Her son replied, **"Yes, I'm here. I'm alive. Take courage to live on, to wait until the time comes when you will join father and me. We'll meet again, and in the meantime I'll help you in every way in my power."**

She did not hear his voice, but she became calmer

and he realized that some measure of comfort had been conveyed from his mind to hers.

Later, when Geoffrey's mother came to Mrs. Leonard, he was eventually able to communicate his whole story to her and to reassure her even further. He told her then of all the interesting and exciting activities he was engaged in, in the spirit world. He explained to her that **her excessive grief was the one thing that prevented him from being completely happy in his new life**.

Geoffrey's story gives support to Sir Oliver Lodge's appeal to all bereaved persons: **"Though it is natural for you to grieve, to miss the physical presence of those whom you love, you must remember that in the early days of their new life on the other side, their happiness is in your hands. They know you will miss them, but they are able to see you often even though you are blind and deaf to their presence. The more hopefully and happily you are able to regard the time that must elapse before you can see them again, the more easily they can take up their new lives, unburdened by anxious care for you and your sorrows."**

How to help the newly departed

Believe it or not, you can be of assistance to those who have recently died.

This chapter explores the nocturnal out-of-body experience (OBE), how you can help the departed during sleep, and ways to help them while you're awake.

The nocturnal OBE

When we sleep, our souls leave our bodies to experience adventures on what is called the astral plane (see "Where do we go when we die?" on page 21). This section discusses:

- Whom we can help
- What part of us leaves the body during sleep
- Where we go when we're sleeping
- What happens when someone dies
- Where departed souls go

Note: Much material for this article comes from Robert Crookall's research results published in *During Sleep* (University Books, 1974).

Whom we help while we sleep

Many people, especially those who are psychically sensitive, can help the following types of individuals during their sleeping hours:

- Other living people
- Those who are dying
- Those who have just died (the "newly dead")
- Earthbound spirits (the dead who cling to the earthly plane instead of advancing into the higher spiritual realms)

What part of us leaves the body?

Human beings are the union of spirit and matter.

Our non-physical form consists of *energetic layers* that can separate from the physical shell during sleep (also during waking OBEs and near-death experiences).

These layers are shown in the following chart, starting with the physical body at the bottom.

Just as your physical body contains all of the energetic layers, each successive layer or body contains the higher bodies—kind of like those nesting Russian *matryoshka* dolls.

Your etheric body energizes and maintains your physical body, but it is *not* a vehicle of consciousness. Therefore, if your etheric body separates from your physical body, your out-of-body travel will be limited to the etheric realm, which is closest to earth. If so, what you see on this plane will be cloudy and dim. In this realm are the newly dead, who have vacated their physical bodies but are still ensheathed in their etheric vehicles.

Layer	Body	
7th	Ketheric	Spiritual
6th	Celestial	
5th	Higher Mental	
4th	Astral	Soul
3rd	Lower Mental	Earthly
2nd	Emotional	
1st	Etheric	
—	Physical	

Why we don't remember our sleep travels

The astral body (soul) is our primary vehicle of consciousness. But when it is out of the body, we usually don't remember what we experience. This is because they are soul-body activities.

> During sleep, it is possible that you have visited the spheres whilst your physical body lay dormant. Temporarily released from four-dimensional captivity, you have enjoyed, for a while, the companionship of your beloved. Alas, upon awakening, the remembrance of the astral experience has failed to register. … But the spirit,

the larger personality does not forget.

—Sylvia Barbanell, *When a Child Dies*

To remember our astral travels during our waking hours, they must somehow pass through the *brain* of the physical body. Crookall states that the experiences we observe in the body pass through our physical brain, and these we can remember both during our waking hours and when our soul is out of our body.

What we experience while out of the body our soul may remember, but our brains naturally cannot. This is why dreams (memories of astral travel) often fade soon after waking.

To remember your nocturnal soul travels, make the habit of setting your intention to recall them as you are falling asleep.

Metaphysical magician W. E. Butler explains in *The Magician: His Training and Work*, that

> To remember, or 'bring through' the recollection
> of an astral plane activity, it is necessary to so work
> upon the etheric body, that a certain amount of
> its substance vibrates in harmony with our astral
> consciousness. When this has been done, then it
> is possible to induce in the physical brain some
> memory of what has been seen and done on the
> inner planes, though since inner plane experiences
> are not of the material order, it will be found almost
> impossible to bring through a full realisation of
> such experiences; the essence will usually escape us.

Where we go when we leave the body during sleep

The seven spiritual bodies of the human being roughly correspond to the spiritual planes of existence. (For a diagram of these realms, see "Where do we go when we die?" on page 21.) The physical or material world, corresponding to the physical body, is encased in the etheric realm, which pertains to the etheric body.

When our higher form leaves our physical and etheric bodies behind (during sleep, a waking OBE, an NDE, or at death), we enter the astral realm.

What happens when we die

The typical events that happen when we die are outlined in "Where do we go when we die?" on page 21.

When the physical body dies, the energetic bodies are released. Sometimes the soul (astral) and higher bodies remain contained within the etheric body. This ensheathment could last for a few hours or a few days.

During this time, psychically sensitive persons may glimpse the newly dead in their etheric body. From the point of view of the dead, the spirit world looks hazy, and they are unable to progress into the astral realm until they shed the etheric vehicle. When they do, the discarded etheric body decays and its atoms dissolve into the etheric realm for use elsewhere.

During and after the process of death, spirit helpers are present to help transition new arrivals into the astral realm.

Where the soul ends up

If the soul led an exceedingly negative life or formed unhealthy attachments to the earth plane, its activities, or its inhabitants, it may find itself in the lower astral realms ("The lower astral levels" on page 22). **Some may get stuck in the lower realms because of misconceptions about the afterlife or because they refuse help from guides who do not meet their expectations.**

If these individuals are able to work through their issues and misguided beliefs, let go of negativity and material attachments, and receive the assistance of the higher beings sent to help them, they may progress to the higher astral realms. This is called "going toward the light."

Most souls find themselves in the mid astral planes ("The middle astral levels" on page 23). But those individuals who seem to have lost their way or are for some reason unable to go higher need help to adjust to the afterlife and make progress in the astral planes.

This is where you come in. **You can help them while you sleep.**

How you can help the departed during sleep

You may volunteer during your sleeping hours to help the newly departed "cross over" into the higher realms. You could do this on your own. You can also team up with others to do this work.

You can cooperate with discarnate souls in the mid astral realms to help the newly dead—or those who are stuck in the lower realms—to rise higher.

Have you ever dreamed of a loved one who has died?

It may not be a dream. It could be an actual meeting on the astral planes, which you can visit when your body is asleep. Why is sleep a good time to contact those on the other side?

> [P]arapsychological research indicates psychic abilities are enhanced by [altered states of consciousness], such as the cusp of sleep (whether just waking up or falling asleep), dreams, meditation, hypnotic trance, and partial sensory deprivation, to name just a few. In addition, the rational, skeptical part of the mind is on break, preventing it from interfering.
>
> —Pamela Rae Heath and Jon Klimo, *Handbook to the Afterlife*

How do we help the dead while we sleep? Annie Besant advises, **"Think of your loved dead, fix your mind on them, and in the hours of [bodily] sleep, ... you shall be with them and may give them much help."**

As you are falling asleep, think of a recently deceased loved one, or of helping such souls in general. Couple these thoughts with a desire to help them progress. Keep at it successive nights, and then pay attention to the dreams that wake you.

> There are no special tricks for receiving the dead in your dreams other than to know that it happens and be open to the experience. You can mentally ask them to come visit as you fall off to sleep. If you like using visualization, you can even imagine setting up your kitchen table with some coffee or tea and cookies and opening the door, specifically inviting whom you want to come see you.

The real trick is not so much to get them to come
as to remember it afterward. As with any dream
work, it helps to keep a pen and pad of paper by
your bedside, so you can write down what you
remember the moment you wake up, without delay.

—Pamela Rae Heath and Jon Klimo, *Handbook to
the Afterlife*

Team up with the departed to help those crossing over

It's easier for the living to remain close to the earth realm,
where newly departed souls enter the afterlife. Therefore, you
could team up with those who have recently died to help others who are crossing over. This is especially helpful for those
who have died suddenly, unprepared.

**Such teams assist newly dead souls to understand where
they are and what's happened to them. They also help to
locate and enlist the aid of souls in the higher realms
who cannot draw as near to the earth plane to receive
newcomers.**

These deliverance teams run an "escort service," so to
speak, educating and leading the newly dead toward the
planes of light. The living and the recently departed help
other newcomers by connecting them with the spirits on the
higher planes, who then receive them and take them higher.

If this interests you, in your prayers and before you go to
sleep, express your desire to be part of this group of helpers.

Why are the living and the recently dead better able
to help those crossing over than are the inhabitants of the
higher astral realms?

The etheric bridge

In *The Life Beyond Death with Evidence*, Rev. C. Drayton Thomas explains that, "It is a no-man's land between the two conditions." By two conditions he means the mortal, physical world, and the heavenly realm, or higher astral planes.

For living earth people to communicate with people in Spirit, they must connect through the bridgeway of their etheric body ("What part of us leaves the body?" on page 36).

The etheric body enables them to hang out on the borderline between the realms of matter and Spirit. Crookall confirms this:

> The etheric body is a necessary link or bridge
> between the living (who use a physical body) and
> the normal dead (who have shed the etheric and
> use only the soul body).
>
> —Robert Crookall, *During Sleep*

The living are better able to communicate with the dead

Earthbound spirits reside neither in the physical world nor the higher astral planes. Crookall explains that it's difficult for spirits in the higher astral planes to "penetrate the shell of thoughts of an earthbound spirit."

> But if a mortal who is psychically sensitive will help
> the earthbound spirit to understand that there is a
> higher state for them, and encourage them to reach
> for it, they may be helped—and put themselves

within the realm where those spirits who dwell
higher may receive them and bring them up.

—Robert Crookall, *During Sleep*

Since the living still possess an etheric body, they may act
as the staff of a "halfway house" during their sleeping hours.
**They're better at communicating with and helping the
newly dead who are still earthbound because they have not
yet shed their etheric bodies.**

The soul body is connected to the physical body through
what is called the "silver cord"—the energetic bridge to the
etheric body. Because of this connection, the living feel more
familiar to those who have just crossed over.

Crookall explains further:

> The body of those who have just died includes
> not only the astral or soul body, but it is still
> ensheathed in the etheric body, which is a link or
> bridge between the soul (the instrument of thought,
> will, and emotion), and the physical body (the
> instrument of physical action). As long as the newly
> dead retain their etheric shell, they are easily affected
> by the thoughts and feelings of the living, because
> they also have etheric bodies. Angels*, and humans
> who have shed their etheric bodies and crossed over
> entirely to Paradise conditions [mid or upper astral
> planes], no longer possess this bridge and therefore
> find it difficult to impress and help the newly dead.
>
> If you want to be of service to God, pray that you
> may be able to cooperate with the receiving angels*
> to help the newly dead shed their etheric sheaths and
> cross over completely to Paradise. We are needed to

lift passing souls into the arms of the angels*.

—Robert Crookall, *During Sleep*

*By "angels" here, Crookall means departed humans who have crossed over into the higher astral realms.

How we can work with the angels

Mediums Doris and Hilary Severn asked an earthbound spirit, "Why come to us? Why not ask the angels [for help]?" The spirit answered, "Where are the angels? We have not seen any! You are nearer to us." (*The Next Room*)

Although the "angels"—departed souls in the mid astral realms—are seeking those in the lower astral planes, sometimes (although rarely) the newly dead cannot find them. The recently departed are closer to living humans who are psychically sensitive.

We can help the newly dead to look toward the light, and we can help direct those who have fully crossed over to find these lost souls.

> Coming from the earth plane, and because we mortals have a spirit nature that is nearer to the physical than spirits in Paradise, the higher souls can use the living to create a chain from the higher realms to the lower.
>
> —Robert Crookall, *During Sleep*

If you want to help the newly dead, set your intention to help them during the hours of sleep.

Helping the dead while you're awake

There are a number of ways you can help lost or troubled spirits in the afterlife.

- You can provide reassurance and explanations to orient the newly dead to their new situation.
- You can pray for them to progress toward the higher realms.
- You can invite them to study about the afterlife with you.

Heath and Klimo explain that anyone can help the newly dead:

> Although having a developed psychic ability enhances your effectiveness and gives you more options for helping spirits, there are some methods—such as prayer or a one-way conversation explaining what happened to the dead—that can be used by everyone, regardless of talent.
>
> —Pamela Rae Heath and Jon Klimo, *Handbook to the Afterlife*

Providing reassurance to the newly dead

A common reason why spirits get stuck on the earth plane is fear. Sometimes they believe they will be judged harshly by God. Others simply don't know what to expect on the other side, so they cling to what they know: the earth realm.

Therefore, **what the newly dead often need is simple reassurance**. Some newly departed do not accept that they are in fact dead. If not, they may reject the spirit helpers who come to assist them and will instead turn to the living for help and comfort.

Heath and Klimo claim that you don't need to be psychic to help in this way. "Just be calm and reassuring as you explain (whether out loud or in thoughts) what is going on, and how the dead can look for others around them in spirit who are trying to help them."

The death and crossing over process is discussed in "What happens when you die" on page 17.

You can also recommend to them that they pray for those in the higher realms to come and find them. Spiritualist John Wadsworth claims that, "If they call for help, the prayer makes a sort of path upon which [higher spirits] can find them" (*A Guide Book to the Land of Peace*).

Praying for the dead

Prayer is very helpful to those in the afterlife.

When asked about what could be done to aid a soul, medium George Anderson once said, "You are already helping your friend more than you know by praying or thinking about him, which sends spiritual 'hugs' to the hereafter" (Anderson and Barone, *Walking in the Garden of Souls*, Berkeley, 2001).

Medium P. M. H. Atwater was often told that prayer is seen by the departed as beams of light that reach them with tangible help (Heath and Klimo).

Crookall explains that the newly dead need our prayers just as the living do. He says, "Religion has taught that when people die, the ties with their surviving loved ones are basically severed, and those who are left no longer have any power to help those who have crossed over. This is unfortunate because it is not true."

We can help the recently departed by praying for them. The dead who have crossed over into the higher astral realms do what they can, but they need our help. "By praying for the newly dead—sending instructive, helpful thoughts—we can help the angels in their task of welcoming the dead into Paradise" (Robert Crookall, *During Sleep*).

Hereward Carrington, in *Your Psychic Powers* (1925), states that:

> Many of the "spirits" who have passed over, being nearer earth than "Heaven" mid astral realms, soon after their transition, are more easily reached by the living than by other spirits—so far as comfort, advice and assistance are concerned—and, for this reason, **prayers of the living are often a great help to those who have recently "passed over"** and are extremely earthbound by reason of their mental and moral characteristics.
>
> —Hereward Carrington, *Your Psychic Powers*

Olive Pixley shares the story of someone in Spirit who reveals the power of prayer:

> "I never knew what prayer was before I came here. It is the force that operates in my world, as electricity does in yours. Prayer materially alters our conditions. When you pray for those who have passed on it is like giving them presents: you alter conditions that can be changed only by the force of prayer."
>
> —Olive C. B. Pixley, *Listening In* (1928)

Studying the afterlife with the departed

Crookall suggests that you can be of the most help to loved ones who have passed on by familiarizing yourself with spiritual truths about the afterlife. How to do this? Reading this book and the books referenced here is a good start!

Many earthbound spirits return to earth and strive to gain from earthly teachers what they failed to learn when they were living. Those souls who did not learn their lessons while they lived in the body are distressed to cross over and find out the spiritual reality that their lives have brought them to.

—Robert Crookall, *During Sleep*

When you sit down to study, issue a mental call to your loved ones to come and study with you. In this way, they may also learn about the realities of the afterlife and how to meet its challenges.

Conclusion

The newly dead sometimes pass into the spirit world not knowing how to cross over into the higher realms. We who are living are often better able to help them find their way to the light.

We can help them while we sleep by determining to visit them in our dreams. We can also help them while awake by providing reassurance to them about their new state, by praying for them using constructive thoughts, and by inviting them to study about the truths of the afterlife with us.

There is abundant evidence to show that the departed are in some instances helped and enabled to make their first advance in the spirit world not so much by angel ministry as by the sympathy, forgiveness and prayer of those still in this mortal life.

—Rev. C. L. Tweedale, *Man's Survival After Death*

Set your intention to help those who are crossing over. When it is your turn to follow the way of all the living, you will ensure a warm welcome into the afterlife.

If this book has helped in your understanding of the crossing over process, or you have an experience to share, I'd love to hear your story. For my contact information, see "About the author" on page 55.

Prayer to St. Michael the Archangel

In times of stress or if you encounter difficult interactions with lingering spirits or negative energy, pray this prayer for Archangel Michael to defend and protect you.

Saint Michael the Archangel, defend us in battle.

Be our protection against the wickedness and snares of the devil.

May God rebuke him, we humbly pray;
and do Thou, O Prince of the Heavenly Host—
by the Divine Power of God—
cast into hell, satan and all the evil spirits,
who roam throughout the world seeking the ruin of souls.

Daily prayer and meditation

Here are two uplifting meditations for the start and end of your day. Envision these things as you pray.

> The light of God surrounds me.
> The love of God enfolds me.
> The power of God protects me.
> The presence of God watches over me.
> Wherever I am, God is. And all is well.
>
> —James Dillet Freeman

> Lord, bless me, and keep me;
> Lord, make Your face shine upon me,
> And be gracious to me;
> Lord, lift up Your countenance on me,
> And give me peace.
>
> —Numbers 6:24–26, modified

About the author

Photo by Jill Bornand

Lee Allen Howard has practiced and studied Pentecostal Christianity and Spiritualism for many years.

He earned a master's degree in biblical studies, pastored a house church for three years, graduated from the Morris Pratt Institute, and became an ordained Spiritualist minister through Fellowships of the Spirit in Lily Dale, New York.

Lee also writes biblical teaching books and supernatural fiction. He's been a professional writer and editor of both fiction and nonfiction since 1985.

You may contact Lee at:

https://leeallenhoward.com/contact-lee/

Follow him on Twitter @LeeAllenHoward.

The best thing you can do for a writer whose book you enjoyed is to write a brief review on Amazon. Thanks for your support!

Supernatural fiction
by Lee Allen Howard

DEATH PERCEPTION – a novel

Kennet Singleton cremates the dead—and then they speak… "Avenge us!"

"Dastardly devious, cleverly conceived, and just a whole lot of fun to read, *Death Perception* is Lee Allen Howard on fire and at his finest. Rife with winsome weirdness, it's like the mutant stepchild of Carl Hiaasen and Stephen King, mixing a truly unique paranormal coming-of-age story with a quirky cast of offbeat noir characters into a novel that's simply unforgettable… and hilariously original. A supernatural crime story, blazing with creative intrigue… don't miss it."

—Michael A. Arnzen, author of *Play Dead*

Nineteen-year-old Kennet Singleton lives with his invalid mother in a personal care facility, but he wants out. He operates the crematory at the local funeral home, where he discovers he can discern the cause of death of those he cremates—by toasting marshmallows over their ashes.

He thinks his ability is no big deal since his customers are already dead. But when his perception differs from what's on the death certificate, he finds himself in the midst of murderers. To save the residents and avenge the dead, Kennet must bring the killers to justice.

> "Lee Allen Howard is quickly becoming a huge favourite of mine. He crafts his characters so well and gives them depth, flaws and realism that you expect from a much more seasoned writer. ...*Death Perception* is smart, funny, engaging, and endearing. A true work of art."
>
> —Malina Roos

DESPERATE SPIRITS
– a duo of supernatural thrillers

If you like crime and mystery with a supernatural bent, succumb to the call of *Desperate Spirits*!

In this short-story duo of supernatural thrillers, Calvin Bricker deals with desperate spirits right in his own neighborhood of McKeesport, Pennsylvania.

In **"The Vacant Lot,"** a supernatural presence beckons from the empty neighborhood lot. Calvin's curiosity leads him to an aged portrait painter with a terrible secret about a dead undertaker and his missing wife, who seeks eternal release.

In **"How I Was Cured of Naïveté,"** a seemingly innocent spirit appears in the foyer of Calvin's home. When he discovers her fate, he sets her free—only to find that little girls aren't always made of sugar and spice. *Snick, snick!*

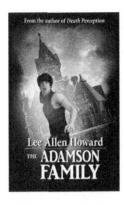

THE ADAMSON FAMILY
– a young adult Gothic novel

Is this house haunted?

There's a creepy old house in the neighborhood. Even in 1977, everyone still says it's haunted. Fifteen-year-old Rendo Flex doesn't believe it—until he sees the face in the window.

Already struggling with the stigma of an institutionalized mother, Ren is tormented by his older sister, Calista, who is following their mother's path toward mental and emotional instability. Why must he suffer for his family's dysfunction?

When Mom wants to leave the psychiatric halfway house for her first family visit in eight years, Ren decides to run away. That's when he glimpses the ghostly face in the tower window...

Made in the USA
Monee, IL
31 March 2023

31003784R00049